When all you have is God and a piece of paper

This devotional journal is for the girl, who no fault of your own, experienced trauma in life earlier than one would expect or be prepared for. The purpose of this devotional is to use therapeutic ideas and biblical truths to show you that despite the pain, trails and challenges, there is hope! Healing is a journey. There is hope for you to have a life filled with love and wholeness.

Trauma amongst the other terms used throughout this devotional are culturally popular, trending and are thrown around loosely. My goal is to educate, encourage and empower you.

It is important that we differentiate facts vs feelings. Trauma is a powerful emotional response to a distressing event. This is a perceived or real threat to life such as war, an accident, being a victim of a crime, an unexpected loss of a loved one, or abuse. The experience of trauma is unique in which it has lived internal responses and symptoms. Trauma is not a situation of being challenged, having strict parents/guardians, being told something you don't want to hear, having to follow rules or protocols you don't like nor understand, living in poverty (in itself) or being lied to. Now, I don't want to minimize or downplay these things. Yes! These are/were real and hurtful; so, your feelings are valid. Going through hardships affects us all differently. Therefore, this journey devotional will hopefully help YOU, and together we will begin the process of healing by exploring the truths through the word of God.

The journey of healing is personal. Situations effect each of us differently. Just because someone else who shared the same experience hasn't responded the same way you have, doesn't make you weak or wrong! It may not look like someone who has experienced similar trials. it takes time. it takes patience and it takes work.

This Devotional is a start to doing the Work. using the unchanging word of God as your foundation. so be kind to yourself and trust that God got you.

I encourage you to use the succeeding journal. To process your emotions, explore ideas, to vent your frustration, track your successes or to help you simply cope in this season

Love to ♥ always,
Jae

If this devotional journal was a gift and/or you don't have a personal relationship with God through his son Jesus Christ, but you are ready to live a life in accordance to his word and have a personal relationship with God, Recite this aloud and believe in your heart, This Prayer for Salvation:

Dear Heavenly Father,

Thank you for your Love, for bringing me to this moment, for touching my heart, to desire the beginning of salvation. A personal relationship with you in this life and with you in heaven when I die. I come to you seeking your forgiveness for my sins, I ask that you come into my life to save me, change me and direct my life by the power of the holy spirit. The bible says that if I confess with my mouth, Jesus is Lord, and believe in my heart that you loved me so much that you sent your son Jesus Christ to die on the cross for my sins and you raised Jesus from the dead, I will be saved. For it is with my heart that I believe and justified, and it is with my mouth that I confess and shall be saved. Thank you, father, In the precious name of Jesus Christ. Amen

Past Mistakes

DAY 1

The expression hindsight is 20/20; meaning perfect vision, is a saying that has always put things into perspective for me. In the moment we don't see all the angles, don't have all the information, and therefore make the best or poor decision with the knowledge we have at that time. We have to stop tearing ourselves down about choices we coulda, woulda, shoulda have made. It happened! There is nothing that can change the order of events. The emotions and pain that have derived from those events are real and true to you! However, in order to overcome perspective is key! Let's reframe our thinking. Explore what God is preparing you for? What lessons could be learned? What positives came out of such an ugly situation? How can you use those events to make changes and apply them to future similar situations? Whose life can be changed by sharing your story or helping them through similar battles? Now let's talk about if you have found yourself making the same mistakes over and over. This is an opportunity for you to explore, why? Are you making decisions based on raw emotions? Are you making impulsive decisions or a combination? Either way, invite God in. Ask God to provide you with wisdom and insight to the patterned behaviors. Be prepared when God reveals them to you.

Biblical Truth:

18 "Forget the former things; do not dwell on the past. 19 See, I am doing a new thing! Now it springs up; do you not perceive it? I am making a way in the wilderness and streams in the wasteland: Isaiah 43:18-19 NIV

13 Brothers and sisters, I do not consider myself yet to have taken hold of it. But one thing I do: Forgetting what is behind and straining toward what is ahead, 14 I press on toward the goal to win the prize for which God has called me heavenward in Christ Jesus. Philippians 3:13-14 NIV

Journal prompt: What is something you can see clearly now from your past that when you were IN it thought you would never make it through.

The Fatherless

Whether you dont know him (your biological father), never met him, dont have the option to know him or an array of other reasons outside your control, not having a consistent and active father in your life does not have to define you. According to the U.S. Census Bureau, 18.4 million children, 1 in 4, live without a biological, step, or adoptive father in the home. According to the national fatherhood initiative, children in homes without a father are:

- 4x Greater Risk of Poverty,
- More Likely to have Behavioral Problems,
- 2x Greater Risk of Infant Mortality,
- More Likely to Go to Prison, More Likely to Commit Crime,
- 7x More Likely to Become Pregnant as a Teen,
- More Likely to Face Abuse and Neglect,
- More Likely to Abuse Drugs and Alcohol,
- 2x More Likely to Suffer Obesity,
- 2x more Likely to Drop Out of School.

I can't tell you how to take that information, but knowledge is powerful. Use this knowledge to reject any thought that you are alone.

Now if any of these statistics apply to you, it's OK. The more important question, is this where you want to remain? Don't use this as an excuse to why you can't do something different in your life. Your mother and father's choices do not fall on you. When you take ownership over your life and allow God's Will and word to prevail, it is more than possible to thrive. I must remind you; mortal man has and will forever be flawed. Your Heavenly Father is without imperfection, he is who you can count on.

Biblical Truth:

Don't you believe that I am in the Father, and that the Father is in me? The words I say to you I do not speak on my own authority. Rather, it is the Father, living in me, who is doing his work. John 14:10 NIV

Defend the weak and the fatherless; uphold the cause of the poor and the oppressed. Psalm 82:3 NAS

Motherless

DAY 3

There are many versions of motherhood. Mothers who are absent, deceased, or present but have a journey of healing to do themselves. Sometimes we are angry, embarrassed, or saddened with the version of a mother we have. Some may compare and wish for an idea of motherhood that is often only seen in movies.

There was a period in my life when I didn't understand my mother's choices and didn't agree with them. It caused unwarranted conflict. It wasn't until I learned of her past pains and loss that I truly understood. God will take your story and use it for HIS glory. To use you as a vessel to help not only peers but your children and their children. One thing I know that I know about God is that HE has always had my back, front and side....

be content with such things as you have. For He Himself has said, "I will never leave you nor forsake you." So we may boldly say: "The LORD is my helper; I will not fear. What can man do to me?" Hebrew 13- 5-6 NKJV

Your version of a mother may not look like what you thought it should, but he will/has placed a woman in your life to help guide, teach, and shape you. Whether that may be a teacher, auntie, bonus mom, or even strangers who become more, they are placed in your life for a reason to fulfil and ordained purpose. Reflect on your life who God has sent you and give thanks.

Biblical Truth:

3 Likewise, teach the older women to be reverent in the way they live, not to be slanderers or addicted to much wine, but to teach what is good. 4 Then they can urge the younger women to love their husbands and children, 5 to be self-controlled and pure, to be busy at home, to be kind, and to be subject to their husbands so that no one will malign the word of God. Titus 2:3-5 NIV

Pure and genuine religion in the sight of God the Father means caring for orphans and widows in their distress and refusing to let the world corrupt you. James 1:27 NLT

Journal prompt: Who is the woman in your life that has positively impacted you? How will you honor her in your actions?

DAY 4

Choices

As a mentor, staff at Residential treatment center, case manager, or counselor, I understand it's not always a simple thing to just choose right from wrong. We were born of inequity. I understand there are contributing factors as to why we are drawn to a patterned behavior or lifestyle. HOWEVER, I also know the power of the Holy Spirit. In our relationship with God if we ask, he can take a cherished taste of sin and lust from your mouth!

The goal isn't to be perfect; the goal is to make the conscious effort and daily practice of aligning your actions to what is good, God word. Christ gave us the example for he was without sin. But baby!! Listen!! It is not easy but can get easier. We've lived our lives lead by the flesh. It will feel foreign to yield to the Holy spirit. We too often are comfortable in our sin. So, whenever you get sick and tired of going through unnecessary trouble and pain, you will have that ah ha moment. It doesn't have to be this way. God will always make a way out of no way! He is a gentleman; he will not force himself on you! The choice / free will is yours.

Biblical Truth:

"Enter by the narrow gate. For the gate is wide and the way is easy that leads to destruction, and those who enter by it are many. For the gate is narrow and the way is hard that leads to life, and those who find it are few. Matthew 7:13-14 ESV

The god of this age has blinded the minds of unbelievers, so that they cannot see the light of the gospel that displays the glory of Christ, who is the image of God. 2 Corinthians 4:4

Journal prompt: What do you have a desire to change?

PAIN (EMOTIONAL)

I don't know who came up with the bold face lie that just because you are a Christian your life won't have challenges, disappointments, hurts, betrayals, loss and all the things! We don't stop being human just because we accept Christ in our hearts as our savior. We still live in the world with other sinful humans. What sets us apart is when we lean in on your relationship, understand that God is with you. Be okay with not knowing why. God doesn't owe us an explanation on his plans but trust that Gods motives are not to punish you. I want to make it clear sometimes we need Christ and counseling to overcome some of our emotional hurts that run deep. Have faith that God got you!

What to do in the meantime? Take the time to identify the source of your pain. Seeking guidance by talking to a trusted person (someone who is equipped to help you). Another method is to journal it, it is important that you get it out of your head. Putting these thoughts on paper allows you to organize your thoughts/pains and makes them appear manageable. It can minimize the power releasing you.

Biblical Truth:

8We are pressed on every side by troubles, but we are not crushed. We are perplexed, but not driven to despair. 9 We are hunted down, but never abandoned by God. We get knocked down, but we are not destroyed. 2 Corinthians 4:8-9

Journal Prompt: Is there an emotional pain that you are struggling with releasing?

Shame

The Webster dictionary defines shame as: a painful emotion caused by consciousness of guilt, shortcoming, or impropriety (wrong); a condition of humiliating disgrace. Shame can lead to other mental health challenges, including depression and anxiety. It may make it difficult to get close to others. Let's unpack this; why do we feel shame for the things that have happened to us? Why do we take ownership in pain that was afflicted on us? Why do we allow others to dictate what burdens we bare? Why do we forgive others but not ourselves by holding on to shame? If you are living in shame from a specific event or period in your life, I'm asking you to make the decision to release yourself. Talk about those feelings, find a healthier outlet for your emotions (not isolate) and show grace to yourself.

Biblical Truth:

¶"Fear not, for you will not be put to shame; And do not feel humiliated, for you will not be disgraced; But you will forget the shame of your youth, And no longer remember the disgrace of your widowhood. Isaiah 54:4 NASB2020

Journal Prompt: Shame begins with identifying shameful emotions. What are your triggers to these feelings? Give a voice to shame, speak it! Shame derives much of its power from secrecy!

Lets Overcome

Overcoming depression, anxiety, fear, pain, adversity, shyness, imposter syndrome is something we will do throughout our lives. We won't just have an isolated battle and be done. Again, this is a journey. We can see evidence of this when you think back to the things you have already overcome. I'm sure there were moments when you felt you wouldn't see the other side, yet here you are! Bruised and scared but HERE! Another word for overcome is to conquer. Trust and be assured though the battle may appear to be too hard or gone on too long, don't lose sight that God cares about his children. Believe it or not adversity builds resiliency. Resiliency is our ability to advance or withstand adversity. Place your trust in God! Trust that he already has/ will supply you with what you need to claim victory.

Biblical Truth:

Yet those who wait for the Lord Will gain new strength; They will mount up with wings like eagles, they will run and not get tired, They will walk and not become weary. Isaiah 40:31

31 What, then, shall we say in response to these things? If God is for us, who can be against us? 32 He who did not spare his own Son, but gave him up for us all—how will he not also, along with him, graciously give us all things? 33 Who will bring any charge against those whom God has chosen? It is God who justifies. 34 Who then is the one who condemns? No one. Christ Jesus who died—more than that, who was raised to life—is at the right hand of God and is also interceding for us. 35 Who shall separate us from the love of Christ? Shall trouble or hardship or persecution or famine or nakedness or danger or sword? 36 As it is written: "For your sake we face death all day long; we are considered as sheep to be slaughtered." [a] 37 No, in all these things we are more than conquerors through him who loved us. Romans 8:31-37 NIV

Journal Prompt: List the things you have overcome. Be proud of your victories. None are too small.

Punishment

Have you ever heard someone say or you felt like you were being punished by God?! Well, if you have not heard, God does not punish us! That was Old Testament God! Lol!! We see God's wrath multiple times in the Old Testament. I give thanks to the new contract in the New Testament, where we see Jesus Christ being born, dying and resurrecting, for our sins! This does not mean that God does not correct us, just as a parent corrects a child. Can you think of a time when you wanted something or wanted to go somewhere, and your parent/guardian said no or not yet? You were all in your feelings mad or sad in that moment but unaware that they were teaching you a valuable lesson. They were protecting you from something you couldn't see that was dangerous or knew that you weren't prepared to handle that thing. Now in hindsight, it all makes sense.

Please note there is truth to the natural order of our actions. Simply put cause and effect. There are positive and negative consequences to the choices we make. You can't spend all your money on clothes, going out to every event and then question God as to why your lights are cut off. Curse him because YOU ran out of gas in your car or got evicted from your home! We can't procrastinate and mismanage our time then wonder why we feel overwhelmed, failing classes or get fired for being habitually late for work. We must take accountability for our actions and the indirect actions of others, but at no point is God to blame.

Biblical Truth:

My son, do not reject or take lightly the discipline of the Lord [learn from your mistakes and the testing that comes from His correction through discipline];
Nor despise His rebuke,12 For those whom the Lord loves He corrects, Even as a father corrects the son in whom he delights.
Proverbs 3:11-12 AMP

Journal prompt: What are areas you need to be honest with the consequences? What will you do differently moving forward?

Why me?

Have you ever had that moment/s to where you found yourself questioning God and asking him WHY me? If you haven't, keep living. Can I share a hard truth? God doesn't owe us an answer...but through obedience and relationship he will reveal to you why you faced those challenges. Whether it was to prepare you for your future, to help someone coming behind you or if it was a consequence to your disobedience, it will be revealed.

I know its not want you wanted to hear, but sometimes its not what we want but what we need. There is they story in the bible about the man born blind. The disciples ask Jesus if the man sinned or his parents. Jesus replies Neither this man nor his parents sinned,' said Jesus, 'but this happened so that the works of God might be displayed in him (John 9:3).

We don't get the answer as to why he was blind, but his story is written in the bible and used to remind people that God will get the glory in our weakness and shortcoming if we rely on him.

Biblical Truth:

9For God saved us and called us to live a holy life. He did this, not because we deserved it, but because that was his plan from before the beginning of time—to show us his grace through Christ Jesus. 2 Timothy 1:9 NLT

"My thoughts are nothing like your thoughts," says the Lord. "And my ways are far beyond anything you could imagine. 9For just as the heavens are higher than the earth, so my ways are higher than your ways and my thoughts higher than your thoughts. Isaiah 55:8-9

Journal prompt: Go to God with your concerns. Pray that his will be done. Ask him for peace, comfort or whatever you need in this season.

Abandonment

A few synonyms for abandoned are discarded, empty or forgotten. Abandonment may feel like worthlessness, confusion, and loneliness. When we put our faith in man abandonment comes with the territory, Yikes! The thought of that sucks, as we don't expect our parents, a partner, or other important people in our lives to leave us. However, when we place our faith in people our own unsaid or unrealistic expectations leave us with this an emotional scar that can take years to overcome.

If you are here, welcome, you are not alone. Let's work to overcome this. Examine your beliefs about relationships and learn about your attachment style. Find the balance of non-romantic intimacy and independence. Communicate and seek out others with healthy relationships, while practicing self-care habits. Christ and counseling can help you explore the fears that are rooted from your past. Identifying those factors can help minimize the impact and limits in your life

Biblical Truth:

"Be strong and courageous, do not be afraid or tremble at them, for the LORD your God is the one who goes with you He will not fail you or forsake you." Deuteronomy 31:6

For my father and my mother have forsaken (abandon, desert, desolate) me, But the LORD will take me up. Psalm 27:10

Yet if the unbelieving one leaves, let him leave; the brother or the sister is not under bondage in such cases, but God has called us to peace. 1 Corinthians 7:15

DAY 11

Growth – change mindset.

Biologically, we will grow from infancy, toddlers, childhood, pre-teen, teen and on up! Our psychical anatomy will consistently grow and change until we die. That is fixed and will never change. However, what about our mindset? Mindset is our mental attitudes, esteem, beliefs and values. These are varying. Our mindsets can paralyze us, leaving us limited. Stuck believing we will never do this or that because we are not worth it. Yet, a flexible and growing mindset can be the catalyst for us to soar. Being resilient through adversity and unstoppable at developing to reach our goals. I believe, that if you have a negative mindset in a particular area in your life you are not fully trusting and believing God is able. Faith check is necessary. If you recognize an area in your life where you are not relying on God, challenge yourself! You must first have the willingness and desire to make an effort. Try new experiences and listen to different perspectives. Be understanding that things don't always turn out how you want them to, but as an opportunity to learn.

Biblical Truth:

8 Finally, brothers and sisters, whatever is true, whatever is noble, whatever is right, whatever is pure, whatever is lovely, whatever is admirable—if anything is excellent or praiseworthy—think about such things. 9 Whatever you have learned or received or heard from me, or seen in me—put it into practice. And the God of peace will be with you.
Philippians 4:8-9

Journal Prompt: What areas in your life would you like to change your mindset to a positive mindset.

Suicidal Thoughts

Did you know there are different types of suicidal thoughts/ ideations (SI). Passive and active. Passive suicidal thoughts occur when an individual no longer has the motivation to live but does not have a plan to take their life. Passive suicidal thoughts sound like "I just wish I could go to sleep and not wake up," "it would be easier for everyone if I wasn't around," or "I wish that the world just ended tomorrow."

Active suicidal thoughts differ from passive thoughts, in that not only does the person no longer have the motivation to live, and they have a plan to end their life. They may also have the means and access to their plan. Active suicidal ideations sound like "It would be so easy to end my life by ___."

Whether you have experienced one or both, they are serious! It is super important you talk about it with someone, a trusted adult in your life.
Now let's get spiritual!!, THE DEVIL IS A LIAR! Any thought that goes against what Gods word says is a bold face lie!! God tells us throughout the bible that YOU ARE!

1. Free- We know that our old sinful selves were crucified with Christ so that sin might lose its power in our lives. We are no longer slaves to sin. Romans 6:6 NLT

2. Loved- For God so loved the world, that he gave his only Son, that whoever believes in him should not perish but have eternal life. John 3:16 ESV

3. Beautiful- For you created my inmost being; you knit me together in my mother's womb. I praise you because I am fearfully and wonderfully made; your works are wonderful; I know that full well. Psalm 139:13-14 ESV

4. Chosen- For he chose us in Christ before the foundation of the world that we may be holy and unblemished in his sight in love. Ephesians 1:4 ESV

5. Renewed- Therefore if anyone is in Christ, he is a new creature; the old things passed away; behold, new things have come. 2 Corinthians 5:17

6. Sealed with the Holy Spirit- In Him, you also, after listening to the message of truth, the gospel of your salvation—having also believed, you were sealed in Him with the Holy Spirit of promise. Ephesians 1:13

7. COMPLETE- and you are complete in Him, who is the head of all principality and power. Colossians 2:10 10. NKJV

I'm sorry for yelling, but God loves you and so do I! I want you to not just exist but LIVE!! You are worth it -Jae

Suicidal Thoughts Continued

Biblical Truth:

But you will not need to fight! Take your places; stand quietly and see the incredible rescue operation God will perform for you, Oh people of Judah and Jerusalem! Don't be afraid or discouraged! Go out there tomorrow, for the Lord is with you! 2 Chronicles 20:17

I will lie down in peace and sleep, for though I am alone, Oh Lord, you will keep me safe. Psalms 4:8

Journal prompt: writing can be a healthy way to help cope with SI, but here are somethings things to keep in mind;

- *·Let it be natural dialogue, dont force yourself.*
- *·It doesn't have to be perfect, dont put pressure on yourself. it can discourage you.*
- *·Journaling is your safe space. Dont judge your thoughts or be too harsh on yourself.*
- *·Dont use to bring yourself lower. I compare it to when you are sad or listening to a sad song that makes you cry. Dont use writing to hurt yourself.*

Disclaimer: If you're struggling, it's okay to share your feelings, Help is available. Speak with someone today call or text 988, the Suicide and Crisis Lifeline. The Lifeline provides 24-hour, confidential support to anyone in suicidal crisis or emotional distress. If you are worried about a friend's social media updates, REPORT IT. You can also help make a connection with a trusted individual like a family member, friend, spiritual advisor, or mental health professional.

Call 911 in life-threatening situations.

Guilt

Previously we discussed shame. Well guilt is shame's cousin. Guilt is a natural emotion and one that can be a positive motivator in human learning. When the burden of guilt is carried too long it can negatively impact important relationships. So, let's look at this from a perspective. Whether you feel guilty as a result of breaking personal values or morals, different empathetically causing harm to someone, having survivors' guilt, or feeling guilty for societal imbalances, it's okay to feel remorseful and want to make amends as this is actionable. Carrying the emotional burden of guilt with no resolve is unproductive and a waste of time. Talk to someone about it, journal about it or find a healthy outlet to release yourself from this emotional captivity. If you have brought your sin to God and asked for his forgiveness. Why reject Gods mercy by holding on to guilt. Self-harm is not only physically harming yourself but can also be emotional. Release it! God has.

Biblical Truth:

It was for freedom that Christ set us free; therefore, keep standing firm and do not be subject again to a yoke of slavery. Galatians 5:1

Brothers and sisters, I do not regard myself as having taken hold of it yet; but one thing I do: forgetting what lies behind and reaching forward to what lies ahead Philippians 3:13 NASB2020

Journal prompt: Practice self-compassion. What are some areas in your life in which you need to forgive yourself?

Day 14

Self-harm

Did you know self-harm is an indication of emotional distress? It's like a emotional tornado leaving destruction as the "only" result of resolve. Let's explore, what is the name of your tornado and what are the conditions or experiences that can be linked to its formation? Common reasons are to be understood as pressure at school, work, bullying, financial concerns, sexual, physical, or emotional abuse, grieving a loss, breakdown of a relationship and even attention seeking? Whatever the reason, you decided to take things in your own hands. The brief resolve you may feel is fleeting and won't solve the root problem. Take it out of man's hands and give it to God. Trusting that through him and with him, things will get better. He can permanently remove this taste from your mouth.

With Christ and Counseling, relapse can be prevented. In the meantime, some alternatives to tension release ideas are popping rubber band on wrist, using marker or pen to mimic where you would cut, running your hands under cold water or hold ice cubes.

Biblical Truth:

Or do you not know that your body is a temple of the Holy Spirit within you, whom you have from God? You are not your own, for you were bought with a price. So glorify God in your body. 1 Corinthians 6:19-20 ESV

For God gave us a spirit not of fear but of power and love and self-control. 2 Timothy 1:7 ESV

God is our refuge and strength, an ever-present help in trouble. Psalm 46:1 NIV

Journal prompts: Journal the negative statement and thoughts that are a LIE. Counter them with the truth of God's word.

Disclaimer: If you are or someone you know is struggling with self-harm, please tell a trusted individual to get the support you need. You are not alone in this. Help is available. Reach out for help identifying a healthy coping mechanism. Text HOME to 741741. In case of emergency or serious injury call 9-1-1.

Broken

I can't speak to your feeling of brokenness; I can only speak to a shared experience. Brokenness can feel like a shattered version of yourself (own perceived image). There is a separation from the thought of who you were and who you are. A void that can't be placed/named, but the missing is apparent.

Here's a idea. THAT thing was removed for a purpose...you are trying to refill something that God sought to release – it was removed on purpose. That part of you needed to be pruned, reshaped, reintroduced in the season where it will yield God ordained fruit(goodness). Don't fight to find the old piece of you! Ask God for clarity on what HE wants you to replace that void with. Then in the meantime, anticipate the answer. Choose every day to go through your day waiting to hear from God with eagerness. Rely on God for your wholeness.

Biblical Truth:

Now may the God of peace Himself sanctify you entirely; and may your spirit and soul and body be kept complete, without blame at the coming of our Lord Jesus Christ. 1 Thessalonians 5:23 NASB2020

DAY 16

Unloved

Who told you were not worthy or deserving of love? Does this person's words /actions outweigh God's word? It's easier for me to say and you to hear, but to put this in practice or understand despite how you feel is the part where faith walking comes in. Due to mistakes or circumstances where you don't have people or THAT person who doesn't show or tell that they love you, replace those thoughts with truth. God's love is unwavering! This means continuing in a strong and steady way: constant, steadfast. God knows your innermost heart desires. Seek Him and His will, God will place people in your life or give you the opportunity to love as his word instructs us to. As you grow in relation with God, his love will overwhelm you! Glory be to God

Biblical Truth:

15 For this is what the high and exalted One says— he who lives forever, whose name is holy: "I live in a high and holy place, but also with the one who is contrite and lowly in spirit, to revive the spirit of the lowly and to revive the heart of the contrite. Isaiah 57:15

No, in all these things we are more than conquerors through him who loved us. For I am convinced that neither death nor life, neither angels nor demons, neither the present nor the future, nor any powers, neither height nor depth, nor anything else in all creation, will be able to separate us from the love of God that is in Christ Jesus our Lord. Romans 8:37-39

Journal Prompt: Create daily habit of writing and verbally speaking positive affirmations to yourself. Listed are a few examples.

"This too shall pass."
"God loves me; therefore, I am lovable."
"I am not a bad person who deserves punishment."
"I have made good changes in the past. I can do it again."
"People may abandon me, but God never will."
"Today I choose self-love instead of self-hate."
"Insecurity is a thief of joy but it's not going to rob me today."

DAY 17

Unworthy

Some synonyms of unworthy are undeserving, not worthy, not good enough for, ineligible for, unqualified for or unfit for. So, let me ask what circumstance contributed to your feeling of being worth less? Worthlessness, is a feeling that may cause an individual to feel as if they have no significance or purpose. It can have a significant negative effect on emotional health. As we previously discussed, any thought that goes against God's word is a lie. I don't know the who, what, when, where or the why that lead you to feel you don't deserve the promises of God. As this feeling develops from a prolonged state of negative mood, it will take intention and time.

Because of Christ, you have access to the fruit of the spirit. You have a right to love, goodness, peace, gentleness, kindness, joy and so much more. Today, choose to believe that whatever led you to believe you are unworthy is a ploy/trick of the enemy to fool you to not operate or fulfill Gods promises in your life.

BIBLICAL TRUTH:

13For You formed my innermost parts; You knit me [together] in my mother's womb.14I will give thanks and praise to You, for I am fearfully and wonderfully made; Wonderful are Your works, And my soul knows it very well.15My frame was not hidden from You, When I was being formed in secret, And intricately and skillfully formed [as if embroidered with many colors] in the depths of the earth.16Your eyes have seen my unformed substance; And in Your book were all written The days that were appointed for me, When as yet there was not one of them [even taking shape]. 17How precious also are Your thoughts to me, O God! Psalm 139: 13-17 AMP

Blessed is the God and Father of our Lord Jesus Christ, who has blessed us with every spiritual blessing in the heavenly realms in Christ. Ephesians 1:3 ESV

Journal prompt: Think of a time when someone you really care about was feeling unworthy. Consider what you would say to this friend and how you would support them. Now respond to yourself in the same way you do to a darling friend.

DAY 18

Whose Burden

Do you ever think that you shouldn't call someone because you don't want to burden them with what you have going on? That they may have this or that already on their plate and it's not fair for you to vent to them or lean on them for support. Even though they expressed, you can. Let me ask you this. Circle back to previous discussion and the practice of self-compassion. If a friend was going through what you are, would YOU turn them away? Would you tell them you don't want to be bothered? If the answer is no, then why don't you be that kind, compassionate and considerate of yourself?

If God placed people in your life that are a means to support you through the trails of life, don't reject it! Accept it! Heal! So, you can be who you need.

Biblical Truth:

Therefore encourage one another and build one another up, just as you are doing. 1 Thessalonians 5:11

Finally, all of you, have unity of mind, sympathy, brotherly love, a tender heart, and a humble \ mind. 1 Peter 3:8

25 not giving up meeting together, as some are in the habit of doing, but encouraging one another—and all the more as you see the Day approaching. Hebrews 10:25 NIV

Journal Prompt: What do you know about the way you treat yourself? Can you identify times in your past when someone else treated you with such harsh judgement or intolerance?

Hopeless (penny with a hole in it)

DAY 19

I'm sorry to know that even though I don't know you personally, you are going through a tough time. You feel like everything that can go wrong has gone wrong? YOU don't see the light and the end of this long tunnel? No sarcasm, but do you not know that there is nothing that you have experienced that God couldn't handle? My question? Who are you putting your faith in to come out on the other side of the space? If you have gone through what you have and are still here today, why do you believe that you don't have the capabilities to continue? Don't worry about that last question! Let's get to work on moving forward. First, please note that nothing in this world will satisfy a thirst (hopelessness), that only God can quench. I know how those intrusive thoughts make it challenging to see the positives! But faith comes by hearing!

Research in positive psychology shows that people who know their strengths and use them frequently tend to feel happier, hopeful and have better self-esteem. They are also more likely to accomplish their goals. These don't have to be some huge life goal! Baby! It be the goal of just getting out of bed! We can't neglect the small victories. A win is a win! Let's recite some biblical truths, affirmation, list out some of those strengths trusting God.

Biblical Truth:

After you have suffered for a little while, the God of all grace, who called you to His eternal glory in Christ, will Himself perfect, confirm, strengthen, and establish you. 1 Peter 5:10 NASB2020

19 God is not human, that he should lie, not a human being, that he should change his mind. Does he speak and then not act? Does he promise and not fulfill? Numbers 23:19

Journal prompt: Identify and list some of your strengths? listed are a few examples.

- Shares, takes turns, and can compromise
- Puts effort into making friends and keeping them
- Accepts differences in others
- Asks for help when needed
- Accepts personal responsibility for actions (good and bad)
- <u>can apologize</u> when needed
- Has a good sense of humor
- Is honest and trustworthy
- Shows loyalty
- Works hard
- Is resilient
- Shows independence
- Is caring, kind, and empathetic
- Helps others
- Cooperates

The sin of others

The infamous line of non-believers if there was a God then why is there war? Why are there kids/people starving? Why is there poverty? Their ignorance doesn't allow them to see that, we live a world of men, men born of sin (evil or wickedness). In the book of Psalm 51 verse 5 it says Surely, I was sinful at birth, sinful from the time my mother conceived me. Due to man's selfishness, jealousy, pride, greediness and need for power, this darkness clouds our governments, cities, towns, communities, and families.

Anywhere there is man, there is sin. So, if someone's sin has happened to you, that was not Gods doing. Remember God is capable, if you ask. Relieve you from the burden of pain! Not only will you be released but what the enemy meant for evil God will us to minister to others. There are things in life we are not supposed to understand. Why do we need to understand the state of mind of someone capable of doing evil and sometimes unspeakable acts against others? The only thing we need to understand is there are forces beyond our comprehension that are working overtime to keep the people from God's promises. Therefore, when we see cruelty or at the receiving end of a cruel act, remind yourself, BUT GOD!

Biblical Truth:

Instead of your shame you will receive a double portion, and instead of disgrace you will rejoice in your inheritance. And so you will inherit a double portion in your land, and everlasting joy will be yours. "For I, the Lord, love justice; I hate robbery and wrongdoing. In my faithfulness I will reward my people and make an everlasting covenant with them. Isaiah 61:7-8

For we do not wrestle against flesh and blood, but against the rulers, against the authorities, against the cosmic powers over this present darkness, against the spiritual forces of evil in the heavenly places. Ephesians 6:12 ESV

Day 21

Anger

When we hear anger, we automatically think of it in a negative space. If we are made in the imagine of God, the emotion of anger is natural. God showed His anger frfr in the Old Testament. We also seen Jesus expressing anger several times in New Testament. Jesus' expression of anger served a purpose, which edified the kingdom. Anger becomes negative when it isn't controlled and/or accompanied with sin. Uncontrolled anger can be consuming, and it steals our energy. If carried too long, it can wreak havoc in our life internally and externally.

Pre-Christ, I allowed anger to control me. I had no hesitation to yield to the impulsive behaviors in my anger. This resulted in me losing relationships, physical altercations, and property damage. Also, it cost me a lot of money to repair doors, walls and whatever else I smashed. Physically I use to have crippling headaches and blurred vision, which I have no doubt was caused from my anger. I am grateful that God removed the hold anger had on me. I am grateful I yield to the Holy Spirit's conviction. I am grateful for God's grace that I did not receive what I deserved while I was in my anger.

God will use anything he sees fit to personally connect with you. Something that spoke to me was the old saying "uncontrolled, anger is like drinking poison and waiting on someone else to die" When will you make the choice, when will you stop drinking the poison?

Biblical Truth:

My dear brothers and sisters, take note of this: Everyone should be quick to listen, slow to speak and slow to become angry, 20 because human anger does not produce the righteousness that God desires. James 1:19-20

Do not be quickly provoked in your spirit, for anger resides in the lap of fools. Ecclesiastes 7:9

Journal prompt: What are your triggers and warning signs to getting angry? The best way to deal with a trigger is to avoid it. This might mean making changes to your lifestyle, relationships, or daily routine

Forgiveness

Culture tells us to match energy! Do them as they do you! People will use that Old Testament law of eye for an eye! We are not under the Mosaic Law in which this was used. We are under the new contract and Christ tells us to forgive as God forgives us. Forgiveness does not mean condoning or the approval of mistreatment. Nor does it mean forgetting or pretending like the wrongdoing never happened. Forgiveness is rarely a one-time event. Instead, forgiveness means the process of letting go of resentment, anger, and hostility toward someone who treated you unfairly. Even when you are justified in having those feelings, forgiveness isn't for the wrongdoer—it's for you. Much like anger, the burden that comes with unforgiving is emotionally draining and mentally detrimental.

Let me be clear! Forgiveness is not: Reconciliation (repairing or returning to a relationship). Forgetting the injustice. Condoning or making excuses for the person's behavior. Forgiveness is not granting legal mercy to the offender or "letting go" but wishing for revenge. You can't seek peace yet hold on unforgiveness. Choose today, will you continue to live in the bondage of unforgiveness? Be free of it! Take back the power of your emotions. Surrender the pain to God and He will help you through it.

Biblical Truth:

21 Then Peter came to Jesus and asked, "Lord, how many times shall I forgive my brother or sister who sins against me? Up to seven times?" 22 Jesus answered, "I tell you, not seven times, but seventy-seven times. Mark 18:21-22 NIV

"Be kind and compassionate to one another, forgiving each other, just as in Christ God forgave you." Ephesians 4:32

Journal prompt: Is there someone who you need God to help you forgive? Do you hold grudges? How would you feel if God held grudges?

Change is

Do you believe that change is possible in your life? Do you think you are beyond the point of change? Do you think nothing will change about your current situation? Despite what you feel, in reality change is constant. Whether you believe it or not, change is going to happen with or without you. It's up to you if you want to participate and how you respond to it. There is nothing that God can't do. If you truly desire to change your character and beliefs that are against his word, God can change your heart. God can! We can't do this on our own strengths and free will. When you put your trust and faith in God, positive change will happen!

What does this look like? Making the choice to change what you expose yourself to, the types of TV you watch, music you listen to, or even the words you use. Challenge yourself to a set time of changing a habit, to prove to yourself that it is possible. Lean and recite God's word until those things no longer have a hold on you.

When it comes to change in people, that's not in our control and more importantly not our business. Let God be God. Shift your focus off others and inward. Focus on the areas in which you want to see yourself grow, mature and change. Gain insight into your mess. You won't have time to worry about someone else's.

Biblical Truth:

"To put off your old self, which belongs to your former manner of life and is corrupt through deceitful desires, and to be renewed in the spirit of your minds, and to put on the new self, created after the likeness of God in true righteousness and holiness." Ephesians 4:22-24

Journal prompt: What is the scariest part about change?

Violated

DAY 24

Every 68 Seconds, someone in America is sexually assaulted. I would be remised if I created a devotional speaking over Trauma and not speak specially about sexual abuse/assault. I want to call it by its name.

The effects of sexual abuse/assault can result in long-lasting adverse mental health effects if you do not work through the trauma. That's why getting professional help is so important. There isn't a standard for how people respond to this form of trauma. It looks different for everyone; it may even take years before symptoms or behaviors reveal themselves. If you have experienced this form of trauma, you are not alone nor do you have to go through this alone.

You did not deserve it.
It was not your fault.
You are not damaged.
You are valuable!
You are worth being loved.

Biblical truth:

The Spirit of the Lord God is upon me, because the Lord has anointed me to bring good news to the suffering and afflicted. He has sent me to comfort the brokenhearted, to announce liberty to captives, and to open the eyes of the blind. He has sent me to tell those who mourn that the time of God's favor to them has come, and the day of his wrath to their enemies. To all who mourn in Israel he will give: beauty for ashes; joy instead of mourning; praise instead of heaviness. Isaiah 61: 1-3

Retrieved from Rape, Abuse & Incest National Network, https://www.rainn.org/statistics

Depression

Depression is another culturally trending term used in recent years. I want to take my time and place emphasis that being sad or experiencing sadness or low mood is not depression. Sadness is a natural emotion felt when someone experiences a loss, disappointment, problems, or other difficult situations. It comes and it goes. Whereas depression is a mental illness that affects your overall temperament and mood as an individual. Often associated with severe enough symptoms that cause noticeable problems in day-to-day activities, such as work, school, social activities, or relationships with others. Again, even with my generalized description I encourage you not to self-diagnose via Dr Google. Please see a professional and explain to them the symptoms which will allow them to determine if in fact you are experiencing depression.

For those who have a diagnosis of depression, I want to stress, you are not your diagnosis! Do not allow this or any label to dictate your actions or behaviors by limiting them. People who experience depression can still thrive, find joy, and overcome. This is again with Christ & counseling. One strategy to start with is to create regular practice of seeking out the positive perspective, while in the mud. Research proves positive thinking decreases depression.

Biblical Truth:

LORD, how they have increased who trouble me! Many are they who rise up against me. Many are they who say of me, "There is no help for him in God." Selah But You, O LORD, are a shield for me, My glory and the One who lifts up my head. Psalms 3:1-3 NKJV

I have told you these things, so that in me you may have peace. In this world you will have trouble. But take heart! I have overcome the world." John 16:33"

Journal prompt: Do you have coping strategies to help you through your season of depression? (coping skill examples: meditation, problem solving, yoga, deep breathing, mindfulness, distraction, relaxation, walking, crying, practice gratitude, take a walk, Use positive self-talk, social/interpersonal coping, physical activity, keeping a journal)

Fear

Have you noticed the relationship between our fears and the news? It's no secret the news feeds our worries. We are fearful that someone will put a razor blade in candy on Halloween. Stranger danger that a big white creepy van is going to kidnap us, and if you travel abroad, you can wake up with your organs removed. Now though these things may have happened; they are not a rational fear to our everyday experiences. What is the likely hood of these things occurring? We are not going to place ourselves and interact in the "world" where this is likely. If we continue to protect ourselves by being cautious, and making smart decisions, there is nothing to be fearful of.

Now let's get into this internal fear. Think back to being a young child. We'd ride all the rollercoasters, jump right into the pool without any skill of swimming, hold snakes and other reptiles, hurry to try and pet any strange dog, or try anything new without hesitation. It wasn't until someone told us NO! "Watch out"! What if!! No, I'm not saying we disregard the potential dangers of such things, but I'm speaking on the boldness, fearlessness that came with DOING it! Fear is learned, so let's unlearn the fears of those who spoke into our lives based on their own insecurities. Again, we don't disregard wisdom but being mindful of WHO you allow to speak into your life. I wouldn't take someone's advice of telling me not to travel abroad from someone scared to fly in an airplane. I wouldn't take advice from someone about scaling a business from someone who has never had a business. Sometimes we pick up on fears from people who don't put their trust in God. So I say, aht aht!! Put those fears down!

We need not to lean on words or have faith in men, but in God. Let us seek and trust in God. Let us walk in boldness that God will protect us from things we physically fear by providing us wisdom. Let us trust and walk in God's word and his will over our lives about what is possible.

Biblical truths

This is my command—be strong and courageous! Do not be afraid or discouraged. For the Lord your God is with you wherever you go." Joshua 1:9

"I sought the Lord, and he answered me and delivered me from all my fears. Those who look to him are radiant, and their faces shall never be ashamed." Psalm 34:4-5

Journal Prompt: What is fear holding you back from? What are you scared of? Is your fear rational?

The worlds Judgment

DAY 27

If no one has ever told you, baby there is nothing you can't do that someone somewhere is going to say something about you! Don't give them folks that much power over you to control your mood or behaviors? God made each of us unique and can't nobody be a better you! Your experiences and beliefs have you moving, dressing, working, talking, and looking like YOU! Accept those things about yourself. Learn how to love the quirks and uniqueness you are made up of. How? By reminding ourselves that God does not make mistakes, and if you believe anything less about yourself, you are calling God a Liar! Oooooooooooh! I'm telling! No in all seriousness, the world's ruler of expectation isn't fair or just. Only God's gives us the grace and mercy that we deserve.

Be aware that feeling the need for approval and overconcern can be drawn from insecurity. Seeking external approval to fill the holes inside you require internal work and personal validation.

Biblical Truth:

For Adonai Elohim will help. This is why no insult can wound me. This is why I have set my face like flint, knowing I will not be put to shame. Isaiah 50:7 CJB

For am I now seeking the approval of man, or of God? Or am I trying to please man? If I were still trying to please man, I would not be a servant of Christ. Galatians 1:10 ESV

Journal Prompt: Complete sentence stems to be your own cheerleader: something I did well today...I felt proud when...

A love that Hurts

As a child I was exposed to it. Watched and glorified popular movies that showed it. So, by the time I was a teenager I was desensitized to domestic violence. I had a flawed understanding of what romantic love looked like. I accepted disrespectful name calling and controlling behaviors as acts of endearment or excusable when done in anger. I thought lovers' quarrels were normal. Despite my natural physical limitations of being a female, without hesitation would go toe to toe with a man. Hindsight I know it was only God that kept me from serious injury. Not every girl gets the opportunity to have a happy ending.

Dating violence is more than physical, it can also emotional, psychological, sexual, stalking and economic. Unhealthy relationships can start early and last a lifetime. Nearly 20.9% of female high school students and 13.4% of male high school students report being physically or sexually abused by a dating partner. That's millions of young people and those numbers increase in college.

No one enters a relationship with the knowledge that it will include violence. Do not feel ashamed or blame yourself. There is help. There is a way out, you don't have to live in fear. An abuser can change, but it is not your job to be abused until they get help. No risk is greater than your life! If you are the aggressor, there is support for you can learn how to express your emotions in ways that don't evolve harming or manipulating others. Despite your exposure or environment, you are responsible for YOUR own actions. We are not responsible for anyone else's actions! Periodt!

Biblical Truth:

But understand this, that in the last days there will come times of difficulty. For people will be lovers of self, lovers of money, proud, arrogant, abusive, disobedient to their parents, ungrateful, unholy, heartless, unappeasable, slanderous, without self-control, brutal, not loving good, treacherous, reckless, swollen with conceit, lovers of pleasure rather than lovers of God, having the appearance of godliness, but denying its power. Avoid such people. 2 Timothy 3:1-8 ESV

Do you not know that you are God's temple and that God's Spirit dwells in you? If anyone destroys God's temple, God will destroy him. For God's temple is holy, and you are that temple. 1 Corinthians 3:16-17 ESV

Love is patient and kind; love does not envy or boast; it is not arrogant or rude. It does not insist on its own way; it is not irritable or resentful; it does not rejoice at wrongdoing, but rejoices with the truth. Love bears all things, believes all things, hopes all things, endures all things. 1 Corinthians 13:4-7 ESV

For confidential help available 24/7 in the United States, call the National Domestic Violence Hotline at 1-800-799-7233 or visit www.thehotline.org

Protection

Let me tell you something about MY God (because its personal). I know that God will always take care of me. There are unseen dangers we can't even fathom. Every time you make it home at the end of the day is the Lord's protection. As cliché as it sounds, someone did not make it home.

Again, things have and can happen to us! It is not because God dropped the ball or he doesn't care about us. We talked about the choices of others, sin, free will, spiritual warfare. But God! Rest knowing God is with you. He is omnipresent, and everywhere all at once. We have seen in the bible story of Job, despite what it may feel or look like in the moment, God won't put more on us than we can bare. God is not only the protector of our physical, we may still take some tuff hits. However, God is also the protector of our souls. We are on this side of heaven but in a short while, through Jesus we will be healed for eternity.

Biblical Truth:

1The Lord is my Shepherd [to feed, to guide and to shield me],I shall not want. 2He lets me lie down in green pastures; He leads me beside the still and quiet waters. 3He refreshes and restores my soul (life); He leads me in the paths of righteousness for His name's sake. Psalm 23 1-3 AMP

Love, Gods Love.

God Is Love. God loved us before we loved. Before we could ever praise him, in the womb of our mother's mother, he designed the path to lead us to him. God did this not because he had to, needed to, but because he wanted to. He desires us to have a relationship with him. Agape, the type of love in which the way God loves us is without condition. There is nothing we can do to stop God from loving us. No, not even sin! He condemns and hates the sin, but not the sinner. Gods does not think like we think. So, when we get ahead of ourselves and get lost in the idea that we are not loveable, understand that is nothing but the lies of the enemy. I love the bible verse about God knowing the count of the hairs on our heads, its personal. Me, the uniqueness of my being, he loves me. God's love is warm, soothing and leaves me awe struck. God has never and will never leave me or forsake/abandon me. He led you to this devotional, to remind you, he is the Alpha and the Omega. Yet if you whisper, he leans in to hear your prayers. Go to Him and stay in Him, find rest in his holy expression of love.

Biblical Truth:

Love is patient and kind. Love is not jealous or boastful or proud or rude. It does not demand its own way. It is not irritable, and it keeps no record of being wronged. It does not rejoice about injustice but rejoices whenever the truth wins out. Love never gives up, never loses faith, is always hopeful, and endures through every circumstance. 1 Corinthians 13:4-7

But God, being rich in mercy, because of His great love with which He loved us, even when we were dead in our transgressions, made us alive together with Christ (by grace you have been saved). Ephesians 2:4-5

38 For I am convinced that neither death nor life, neither angels nor demons, [b] neither the present nor the future, nor any powers, 39 neither height nor depth, nor anything else in all creation, will be able to separate us from the love of God that is in Christ Jesus our Lord. Romans 8: 38-39 NIV

Journal prompt: Recall a time in your life when you can say that God kept you and his love was reviled to you.

| JAN | FEB | MAR | APR | MAY | JUN | JUL | AUG | SEP | OCT | NOV | DEC |

1 2 3 4 5 6 7 8 9 10 11 12 13 14 15 16 17 18 19 20 21 22 23 24 25 26 27 28 29 30 31

JAN	FEB	MAR	APR	MAY	JUN	JUL	AUG	SEP	OCT	NOV	DEC

1 2 3 4 5 6 7 8 9 10 11 12 13 14 15 16 17 18 19 20 21 22 23 24 25 26 27 28 29 30 31

| JAN | FEB | MAR | APR | MAY | JUN | JUL | AUG | SEP | OCT | NOV | DEC |

1 2 3 4 5 6 7 8 9 10 11 12 13 14 15 16 17 18 19 20 21 22 23 24 25 26 27 28 29 30 31

| JAN | FEB | MAR | APR | MAY | JUN | JUL | AUG | SEP | OCT | NOV | DEC |

1 2 3 4 5 6 7 8 9 10 11 12 13 14 15 16 17 18 19 20 21 22 23 24 25 26 27 28 29 30 31

| JAN | FEB | MAR | APR | MAY | JUN | JUL | AUG | SEP | OCT | NOV | DEC |

1 2 3 4 5 6 7 8 9 10 11 12 13 14 15 16 17 18 19 20 21 22 23 24 25 26 27 28 29 30 31

| JAN | FEB | MAR | APR | MAY | JUN | JUL | AUG | SEP | OCT | NOV | DEC |

1 2 3 4 5 6 7 8 9 10 11 12 13 14 15 16 17 18 19 20 21 22 23 24 25 26 27 28 29 30 31

| JAN | FEB | MAR | APR | MAY | JUN | JUL | AUG | SEP | OCT | NOV | DEC |

1 2 3 4 5 6 7 8 9 10 11 12 13 14 15 16 17 18 19 20 21 22 23 24 25 26 27 28 29 30 31

| JAN | FEB | MAR | APR | MAY | JUN | JUL | AUG | SEP | OCT | NOV | DEC |

1 2 3 4 5 6 7 8 9 10 11 12 13 14 15 16 17 18 19 20 21 22 23 24 25 26 27 28 29 30 31

| JAN | FEB | MAR | APR | MAY | JUN | JUL | AUG | SEP | OCT | NOV | DEC |

1 2 3 4 5 6 7 8 9 10 11 12 13 14 15 16 17 18 19 20 21 22 23 24 25 26 27 28 29 30 31

| JAN | FEB | MAR | APR | MAY | JUN | JUL | AUG | SEP | OCT | NOV | DEC |

1 2 3 4 5 6 7 8 9 10 11 12 13 14 15 16 17 18 19 20 21 22 23 24 25 26 27 28 29 30 31

| JAN | FEB | MAR | APR | MAY | JUN | JUL | AUG | SEP | OCT | NOV | DEC |

1 2 3 4 5 6 7 8 9 10 11 12 13 14 15 16 17 18 19 20 21 22 23 24 25 26 27 28 29 30 31

| JAN | FEB | MAR | APR | MAY | JUN | JUL | AUG | SEP | OCT | NOV | DEC |

1 2 3 4 5 6 7 8 9 10 11 12 13 14 15 16 17 18 19 20 21 22 23 24 25 26 27 28 29 30 31

| JAN | FEB | MAR | APR | MAY | JUN | JUL | AUG | SEP | OCT | NOV | DEC |

1 2 3 4 5 6 7 8 9 10 11 12 13 14 15 16 17 18 19 20 21 22 23 24 25 26 27 28 29 30 31

| JAN | FEB | MAR | APR | MAY | JUN | JUL | AUG | SEP | OCT | NOV | DEC |

1 2 3 4 5 6 7 8 9 10 11 12 13 14 15 16 17 18 19 20 21 22 23 24 25 26 27 28 29 30 31

| JAN | FEB | MAR | APR | MAY | JUN | JUL | AUG | SEP | OCT | NOV | DEC |

1 2 3 4 5 6 7 8 9 10 11 12 13 14 15 16 17 18 19 20 21 22 23 24 25 26 27 28 29 30 31

| JAN | FEB | MAR | APR | MAY | JUN | JUL | AUG | SEP | OCT | NOV | DEC |

1 2 3 4 5 6 7 8 9 10 11 12 13 14 15 16 17 18 19 20 21 22 23 24 25 26 27 28 29 30 31

| JAN | FEB | MAR | APR | MAY | JUN | JUL | AUG | SEP | OCT | NOV | DEC |

1 2 3 4 5 6 7 8 9 10 11 12 13 14 15 16 17 18 19 20 21 22 23 24 25 26 27 28 29 30 31

JAN	FEB	MAR	APR	MAY	JUN	JUL	AUG	SEP	OCT	NOV	DEC

1 2 3 4 5 6 7 8 9 10 11 12 13 14 15 16 17 18 19 20 21 22 23 24 25 26 27 28 29 30 31

| JAN | FEB | MAR | APR | MAY | JUN | JUL | AUG | SEP | OCT | NOV | DEC |

1 2 3 4 5 6 7 8 9 10 11 12 13 14 15 16 17 18 19 20 21 22 23 24 25 26 27 28 29 30 31

JAN	FEB	MAR	APR	MAY	JUN	JUL	AUG	SEP	OCT	NOV	DEC

1 2 3 4 5 6 7 8 9 10 11 12 13 14 15 16 17 18 19 20 21 22 23 24 25 26 27 28 29 30 31

JAN	FEB	MAR	APR	MAY	JUN	JUL	AUG	SEP	OCT	NOV	DEC

1 2 3 4 5 6 7 8 9 10 11 12 13 14 15 16 17 18 19 20 21 22 23 24 25 26 27 28 29 30 31

| JAN | FEB | MAR | APR | MAY | JUN | JUL | AUG | SEP | OCT | NOV | DEC |

1 2 3 4 5 6 7 8 9 10 11 12 13 14 15 16 17 18 19 20 21 22 23 24 25 26 27 28 29 30 31

| JAN | FEB | MAR | APR | MAY | JUN | JUL | AUG | SEP | OCT | NOV | DEC |

1 2 3 4 5 6 7 8 9 10 11 12 13 14 15 16 17 18 19 20 21 22 23 24 25 26 27 28 29 30 31

| JAN | FEB | MAR | APR | MAY | JUN | JUL | AUG | SEP | OCT | NOV | DEC |

1 2 3 4 5 6 7 8 9 10 11 12 13 14 15 16 17 18 19 20 21 22 23 24 25 26 27 28 29 30 31

| JAN | FEB | MAR | APR | MAY | JUN | JUL | AUG | SEP | OCT | NOV | DEC |

1 2 3 4 5 6 7 8 9 10 11 12 13 14 15 16 17 18 19 20 21 22 23 24 25 26 27 28 29 30 31

| JAN | FEB | MAR | APR | MAY | JUN | JUL | AUG | SEP | OCT | NOV | DEC |

1 2 3 4 5 6 7 8 9 10 11 12 13 14 15 16 17 18 19 20 21 22 23 24 25 26 27 28 29 30 31

| JAN | FEB | MAR | APR | MAY | JUN | JUL | AUG | SEP | OCT | NOV | DEC |

1 2 3 4 5 6 7 8 9 10 11 12 13 14 15 16 17 18 19 20 21 22 23 24 25 26 27 28 29 30 31

| JAN | FEB | MAR | APR | MAY | JUN | JUL | AUG | SEP | OCT | NOV | DEC |

1 2 3 4 5 6 7 8 9 10 11 12 13 14 15 16 17 18 19 20 21 22 23 24 25 26 27 28 29 30 31

| JAN | FEB | MAR | APR | MAY | JUN | JUL | AUG | SEP | OCT | NOV | DEC |

1 2 3 4 5 6 7 8 9 10 11 12 13 14 15 16 17 18 19 20 21 22 23 24 25 26 27 28 29 30 31

| JAN | FEB | MAR | APR | MAY | JUN | JUL | AUG | SEP | OCT | NOV | DEC |

1 2 3 4 5 6 7 8 9 10 11 12 13 14 15 16 17 18 19 20 21 22 23 24 25 26 27 28 29 30 31

| JAN | FEB | MAR | APR | MAY | JUN | JUL | AUG | SEP | OCT | NOV | DEC |

1 2 3 4 5 6 7 8 9 10 11 12 13 14 15 16 17 18 19 20 21 22 23 24 25 26 27 28 29 30 31

| JAN | FEB | MAR | APR | MAY | JUN | JUL | AUG | SEP | OCT | NOV | DEC |

1 2 3 4 5 6 7 8 9 10 11 12 13 14 15 16 17 18 19 20 21 22 23 24 25 26 27 28 29 30 31

| JAN | FEB | MAR | APR | MAY | JUN | JUL | AUG | SEP | OCT | NOV | DEC |

1 2 3 4 5 6 7 8 9 10 11 12 13 14 15 16 17 18 19 20 21 22 23 24 25 26 27 28 29 30 31

| JAN | FEB | MAR | APR | MAY | JUN | JUL | AUG | SEP | OCT | NOV | DEC |

1 2 3 4 5 6 7 8 9 10 11 12 13 14 15 16 17 18 19 20 21 22 23 24 25 26 27 28 29 30 31

| JAN | FEB | MAR | APR | MAY | JUN | JUL | AUG | SEP | OCT | NOV | DEC |

1 2 3 4 5 6 7 8 9 10 11 12 13 14 15 16 17 18 19 20 21 22 23 24 25 26 27 28 29 30 31

JAN	FEB	MAR	APR	MAY	JUN	JUL	AUG	SEP	OCT	NOV	DEC

1 2 3 4 5 6 7 8 9 10 11 12 13 14 15 16 17 18 19 20 21 22 23 24 25 26 27 28 29 30 31

| JAN | FEB | MAR | APR | MAY | JUN | JUL | AUG | SEP | OCT | NOV | DEC |

1 2 3 4 5 6 7 8 9 10 11 12 13 14 15 16 17 18 19 20 21 22 23 24 25 26 27 28 29 30 31

| JAN | FEB | MAR | APR | MAY | JUN | JUL | AUG | SEP | OCT | NOV | DEC |

1 2 3 4 5 6 7 8 9 10 11 12 13 14 15 16 17 18 19 20 21 22 23 24 25 26 27 28 29 30 31

| JAN | FEB | MAR | APR | MAY | JUN | JUL | AUG | SEP | OCT | NOV | DEC |

1 2 3 4 5 6 7 8 9 10 11 12 13 14 15 16 17 18 19 20 21 22 23 24 25 26 27 28 29 30 31

| JAN | FEB | MAR | APR | MAY | JUN | JUL | AUG | SEP | OCT | NOV | DEC |

1 2 3 4 5 6 7 8 9 10 11 12 13 14 15 16 17 18 19 20 21 22 23 24 25 26 27 28 29 30 31

| JAN | FEB | MAR | APR | MAY | JUN | JUL | AUG | SEP | OCT | NOV | DEC |

1 2 3 4 5 6 7 8 9 10 11 12 13 14 15 16 17 18 19 20 21 22 23 24 25 26 27 28 29 30 31

| JAN | FEB | MAR | APR | MAY | JUN | JUL | AUG | SEP | OCT | NOV | DEC |

1 2 3 4 5 6 7 8 9 10 11 12 13 14 15 16 17 18 19 20 21 22 23 24 25 26 27 28 29 30 31

| JAN | FEB | MAR | APR | MAY | JUN | JUL | AUG | SEP | OCT | NOV | DEC |

1 2 3 4 5 6 7 8 9 10 11 12 13 14 15 16 17 18 19 20 21 22 23 24 25 26 27 28 29 30 31

| JAN | FEB | MAR | APR | MAY | JUN | JUL | AUG | SEP | OCT | NOV | DEC |

1 2 3 4 5 6 7 8 9 10 11 12 13 14 15 16 17 18 19 20 21 22 23 24 25 26 27 28 29 30 31

| JAN | FEB | MAR | APR | MAY | JUN | JUL | AUG | SEP | OCT | NOV | DEC |

1 2 3 4 5 6 7 8 9 10 11 12 13 14 15 16 17 18 19 20 21 22 23 24 25 26 27 28 29 30 31

| JAN | FEB | MAR | APR | MAY | JUN | JUL | AUG | SEP | OCT | NOV | DEC |

1 2 3 4 5 6 7 8 9 10 11 12 13 14 15 16 17 18 19 20 21 22 23 24 25 26 27 28 29 30 31

| JAN | FEB | MAR | APR | MAY | JUN | JUL | AUG | SEP | OCT | NOV | DEC |

1 2 3 4 5 6 7 8 9 10 11 12 13 14 15 16 17 18 19 20 21 22 23 24 25 26 27 28 29 30 31

| JAN | FEB | MAR | APR | MAY | JUN | JUL | AUG | SEP | OCT | NOV | DEC |

1 2 3 4 5 6 7 8 9 10 11 12 13 14 15 16 17 18 19 20 21 22 23 24 25 26 27 28 29 30 31

| JAN | FEB | MAR | APR | MAY | JUN | JUL | AUG | SEP | OCT | NOV | DEC |

1 2 3 4 5 6 7 8 9 10 11 12 13 14 15 16 17 18 19 20 21 22 23 24 25 26 27 28 29 30 31

| JAN | FEB | MAR | APR | MAY | JUN | JUL | AUG | SEP | OCT | NOV | DEC |

1 2 3 4 5 6 7 8 9 10 11 12 13 14 15 16 17 18 19 20 21 22 23 24 25 26 27 28 29 30 31

| JAN | FEB | MAR | APR | MAY | JUN | JUL | AUG | SEP | OCT | NOV | DEC |

1 2 3 4 5 6 7 8 9 10 11 12 13 14 15 16 17 18 19 20 21 22 23 24 25 26 27 28 29 30 31

| JAN | FEB | MAR | APR | MAY | JUN | JUL | AUG | SEP | OCT | NOV | DEC |

1 2 3 4 5 6 7 8 9 10 11 12 13 14 15 16 17 18 19 20 21 22 23 24 25 26 27 28 29 30 31

| JAN | FEB | MAR | APR | MAY | JUN | JUL | AUG | SEP | OCT | NOV | DEC |

1 2 3 4 5 6 7 8 9 10 11 12 13 14 15 16 17 18 19 20 21 22 23 24 25 26 27 28 29 30 31

| JAN | FEB | MAR | APR | MAY | JUN | JUL | AUG | SEP | OCT | NOV | DEC |

1 2 3 4 5 6 7 8 9 10 11 12 13 14 15 16 17 18 19 20 21 22 23 24 25 26 27 28 29 30 31

| JAN | FEB | MAR | APR | MAY | JUN | JUL | AUG | SEP | OCT | NOV | DEC |

1 2 3 4 5 6 7 8 9 10 11 12 13 14 15 16 17 18 19 20 21 22 23 24 25 26 27 28 29 30 31

| JAN | FEB | MAR | APR | MAY | JUN | JUL | AUG | SEP | OCT | NOV | DEC |

1 2 3 4 5 6 7 8 9 10 11 12 13 14 15 16 17 18 19 20 21 22 23 24 25 26 27 28 29 30 31

| JAN | FEB | MAR | APR | MAY | JUN | JUL | AUG | SEP | OCT | NOV | DEC |

1 2 3 4 5 6 7 8 9 10 11 12 13 14 15 16 17 18 19 20 21 22 23 24 25 26 27 28 29 30 31

| JAN | FEB | MAR | APR | MAY | JUN | JUL | AUG | SEP | OCT | NOV | DEC |

1 2 3 4 5 6 7 8 9 10 11 12 13 14 15 16 17 18 19 20 21 22 23 24 25 26 27 28 29 30 31

___

___

___

___

___

___

___

___

___

___

___

___

___

___

___

___

___

___

___

___

___

___

___

___

| JAN | FEB | MAR | APR | MAY | JUN | JUL | AUG | SEP | OCT | NOV | DEC |

1 2 3 4 5 6 7 8 9 10 11 12 13 14 15 16 17 18 19 20 21 22 23 24 25 26 27 28 29 30 31

| JAN | FEB | MAR | APR | MAY | JUN | JUL | AUG | SEP | OCT | NOV | DEC |

1 2 3 4 5 6 7 8 9 10 11 12 13 14 15 16 17 18 19 20 21 22 23 24 25 26 27 28 29 30 31

| JAN | FEB | MAR | APR | MAY | JUN | JUL | AUG | SEP | OCT | NOV | DEC |

1 2 3 4 5 6 7 8 9 10 11 12 13 14 15 16 17 18 19 20 21 22 23 24 25 26 27 28 29 30 31

| JAN | FEB | MAR | APR | MAY | JUN | JUL | AUG | SEP | OCT | NOV | DEC |

1 2 3 4 5 6 7 8 9 10 11 12 13 14 15 16 17 18 19 20 21 22 23 24 25 26 27 28 29 30 31

| JAN | FEB | MAR | APR | MAY | JUN | JUL | AUG | SEP | OCT | NOV | DEC |

1 2 3 4 5 6 7 8 9 10 11 12 13 14 15 16 17 18 19 20 21 22 23 24 25 26 27 28 29 30 31

| JAN | FEB | MAR | APR | MAY | JUN | JUL | AUG | SEP | OCT | NOV | DEC |

1 2 3 4 5 6 7 8 9 10 11 12 13 14 15 16 17 18 19 20 21 22 23 24 25 26 27 28 29 30 31

| JAN | FEB | MAR | APR | MAY | JUN | JUL | AUG | SEP | OCT | NOV | DEC |

1 2 3 4 5 6 7 8 9 10 11 12 13 14 15 16 17 18 19 20 21 22 23 24 25 26 27 28 29 30 31

| JAN | FEB | MAR | APR | MAY | JUN | JUL | AUG | SEP | OCT | NOV | DEC |

1 2 3 4 5 6 7 8 9 10 11 12 13 14 15 16 17 18 19 20 21 22 23 24 25 26 27 28 29 30 31

| JAN | FEB | MAR | APR | MAY | JUN | JUL | AUG | SEP | OCT | NOV | DEC |

1 2 3 4 5 6 7 8 9 10 11 12 13 14 15 16 17 18 19 20 21 22 23 24 25 26 27 28 29 30 31

| JAN | FEB | MAR | APR | MAY | JUN | JUL | AUG | SEP | OCT | NOV | DEC |

1 2 3 4 5 6 7 8 9 10 11 12 13 14 15 16 17 18 19 20 21 22 23 24 25 26 27 28 29 30 31

| JAN | FEB | MAR | APR | MAY | JUN | JUL | AUG | SEP | OCT | NOV | DEC |

1 2 3 4 5 6 7 8 9 10 11 12 13 14 15 16 17 18 19 20 21 22 23 24 25 26 27 28 29 30 31

| JAN | FEB | MAR | APR | MAY | JUN | JUL | AUG | SEP | OCT | NOV | DEC |

1 2 3 4 5 6 7 8 9 10 11 12 13 14 15 16 17 18 19 20 21 22 23 24 25 26 27 28 29 30 31

| JAN | FEB | MAR | APR | MAY | JUN | JUL | AUG | SEP | OCT | NOV | DEC |

1 2 3 4 5 6 7 8 9 10 11 12 13 14 15 16 17 18 19 20 21 22 23 24 25 26 27 28 29 30 31

Made in United States
Troutdale, OR
08/01/2023

11721004R00060